KENNY
THE HELPER
BEE

BY: KIMBERLY BENHAM

Palmetto Publishing Group, LLC
www.PalmettoPublishingGroup.com

Kenny the Helper Bee
Copyright ©2016 Kimberly Benham

ISBN-13: 978-1-944313-15-9
ISBN-10: 1-944313-15-X

For seeing more in me than I ever saw in myself.
Believing in me, when no one else did.
This is for you mom, love you more!!!

Helper bees were helpful.

They worked all their days.

But one bee named Kenny

Was helpful beyond their ways.

He helped with the gardening and

He helped with the honey.

He helped with the pollen,

Which to bees is worth more than money.

Little Kenny the helper bee

Was often pushed away.

No one wanted to be his friend;

No one wanted to play.

"Get away from us, you teachers' bee!"

"Yeah, you fake bee, you goody two-wings,

Always helping out and

Doing way too many things."

"If you are our friend,

Then slack like the rest.

Don't do your work tomorrow;

Don't do your very best."

Kenny frowned at this,

Knowing not what to do.

Then he heard a voice in his head,

Right there out of the blue.

"That's not why I made you,

Kenny, my helper bee.

You were made to help others

So it would glorify me.

"For I made you, Kenny,

From your head down to your toes.

I made the trees outside

And made the wind that blows.

"I have seen all of your actions

From the very start,

And Kenny, my little helper bee,

It has warmed my heart.

"Remember, everyone is different;

Everyone is unique.

Don't worry about the others—

Only my approval should you seek.

"Go, and think of what I've told you.

Let my truth really sink in.

Stay true on this path I have for you,

And to you I will send a true friend."

"You are the Creator, maker of all.

Without doubt I know it's true.

Would it be okay sometimes

If I sat and talked to you?"

"Any time and always—

If you're lonely or just need to talk,

A shoulder to cry on,

A friend for a long walk.

"Go and be helpful,

My wonderful helper bee,

Knowing how very proud

I am of thee."

As Kenny flew the next day,

The Creator's words fresh in his heart,

He knew that now was the time

For him to do his part:

To be helpful to everyone,

No matter how big or small;

To always be grateful;

To always give his all.

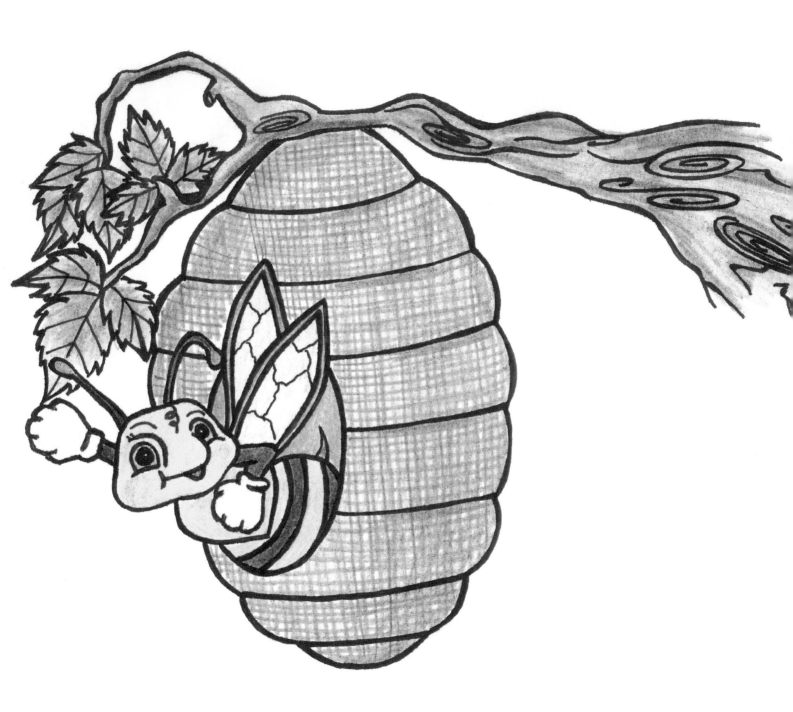

So remember, you can be helpful

Like Kenny the bee, too,

And let the Creator's light

Always shine through you!

About the Author

Kimberly Nicole Benham was born in Atlanta, Georgia, on July 17, 1980. She is the mother of two wonderful, beautiful girls: Andrianna and Briana Renae. Benham teaches at Harvest Christian Academy and is pursuing her bachelor's degree in psychology. With her degree, she hopes to write books with a deeper psychological understanding, teaching children to always love themselves.

Kenny the Helper Bee is her first book.

About the Illustrators

Olga J. Rivera was born in Boston, Massachusetts, and raised in Upstate New York. She served in the Army from 1986 until medically retiring in 2011, earning her veteran title. She is an Art Instructions Schools graduate and has experience working on a plethora of freelance and leisure artistic creations.

Rivera resides in St Mary's, Georgia, where her two children live. She owns one ball python and two sugar gliders. Her aspiration is to someday work with an animal rescue organization.

Jarelie N. McAfee was born in Tacoma, Washington, on June 3, 1990, and was raised in Camden County, Georgia. She earned a bachelor's degree in early childhood education from Valdosta State University and currently works as a pre-kindergarten teacher.

Her love and aptitude for art stem from her parents, Olga J. Rivera and David L. McAfee, who both have artistic backgrounds. McAfee aspires to one day own a business that gives her the chance to try her hand in various artistic endeavors.

Made in the USA
Monee, IL
24 January 2024

51698356R00021